Flute Time 2

Ian Denley

MUSIC DEPARTMENT

OXFORD
UNIVERSITY PRESS

OXFORD
UNIVERSITY PRESS

Great Clarendon Street, Oxford OX2 6DP, England
198 Madison Avenue, New York, NY10016, USA

Oxford is a registered trade mark of Oxford University Press
in the UK and in certain other countries

1 3 5 7 9 10 8 6 4 2

ISBN 0-19-322092-X

Music and text origination by
Barnes Music Engraving Ltd., East Sussex
Printed in Great Britain

CD production by Chapel Digital of Leeds and Andrew King

Photographs by BGA Studios, Hull

Acknowledgements

Any tutor book like this comes about as a result of the efforts of many people, not least the hundreds of
my pupils of differing levels of ability who have, over the years, unwittingly provided excellent material
for these books—my thanks to them.

I would particularly like to thank:

Brenda Dykes, Michael Grocutt, Michael Hodson, Peter Lynch, Margaret Pearson, and Sharon Walker who read
the drafts and made encouraging comments and suggestions; their input was invaluable

Thomas Atkinson, the talented young flute player who appears in the illustrations

Margaret Pearson, for appearing as accompanist, both flute and piano, on the CD

David Blackwell, my editor at Oxford University Press, and his colleagues

Finally, my two teachers, David Butt and Andreas Blau, the long-serving principal flute-players of the BBC Symphony
Orchestra and Berlin Philharmonic Orchestra respectively—both a tremendous inspiration for any student.

CONTENTS

FOREWORD

To you (the pupil)

Welcome to *Flute Time 2*. You are probably around Grade 2 standard by now, so well done!

It's now time to extend the range of notes you know to include the remaining notes of the 3rd octave, as well as the two lowest notes, C and C♯. This is an important time, yet if your embouchure and fingers are working properly, you'll find these notes really exciting, as will your audience!

Take care to learn the high note fingerings correctly. This, together with good breathing and embouchure control, will make all the difference. Keep a steady pace, learn well, and enjoy your flute playing.

To your teacher

Flute Time 2 helps consolidate all the success achieved in *Flute Time 1*.

In this book there is much emphasis on the development of the 3rd octave (right up to top C). This is often a neglected area; after the opening stages, and getting up to high D, pupils tend not to focus on the higher notes as seriously as they did the low register. Yet the complexity of the 3rd octave needs particular care. One issue is that, apart from high D, the fingerings for all these notes resemble their low register counterparts, and it is very tempting (but wrong!) for pupils to try to produce the high register by using low register fingerings and by blowing harder, rather than raising the air-stream.

In reality, most of the high register is based on notes a 12th below; so high E is really an altered low A, high G♯ an altered open C♯, and so on. I have always found this a better way of introducing pupils to the high register, and it seems to avoid bad habits developing. It's also worth remembering that RH–4 stays on the D♯ key for every note of the 3rd octave, right up to and including high A.

Flute Time 2 develops other key aspects of technique and musicianship, including phrasing, more advanced articulation, composing with modes, and development of rhythm. Both forms of the minor scale are used. There are plenty of pieces and studies to play, and further repertoire to complement *Flute Time 2* is included in *Flute Time Pieces*. Appendix I lists further studies which will help consolidate the new points of each lesson.

Take time to go through with your pupil the new information which appears in each lesson, so that they fully absorb each new point before moving on to the next. Check boxes are provided to chart progress.

I hope that *Flute Time 2* will be particularly helpful to all teachers, especially woodwind players who are not flute specialists.

To you both

Pieces with piano accompaniment are presented in two formats on the CD: firstly, a complete performance, then the accompaniment only, with which you can play along; a metronome will count you in when the flute and piano parts start together.

 This symbol (and accompanying track numbers) is placed alongside the notes, exercises, studies, and pieces which appear on the accompanying CD. The first track is the tuning note A. When there are two numbers given in the symbol, the top number indicates the complete performance, and the bottom number the accompaniment alone.

 This symbol indicates which pieces have a piano accompaniment (published in a separate booklet).

All pieces not credited to a composer or marked 'Trad.' and so forth are written by me.

This book is dedicated to David Butt.

Ian Denley
Hull, 2002

The high register (the 3rd octave)

The flute's high register notes sound very brilliant when loud and expressive when quiet, but developing the sort of control needed to achieve this needs a lot of patient practice.

The two most important aspects of producing a healthy high register are:

• a carefully channelled/angled and well-supported air-stream

• absolute accuracy in the fingerings: most of these notes behave badly if not fingered correctly. Every note in the high register is **fingered differently** from the low notes with the same letter-name.

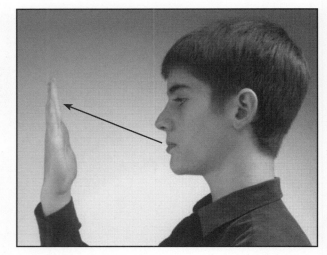

Here is Tom blowing towards his hand, now angling the air towards his finger tips for the high register.

The lower jaw has moved slightly further forward so that the hole between the lips has become smaller, at the same time as sending the air a little higher. Try to keep the lips relaxed, otherwise sound can become taut and you will probably blow sharp.

As before, remember that it is **not** blowing harder—just higher and faster. If you find that you are losing your air quickly, it means that the opening between your lips is too large.

These illustrations show a typical embouchure for the high register. The jaw has pushed the lower lip forwards. Notice how small the opening between the lips is now.

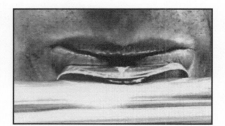

Try to spread the lower lip along the lip-plate—don't smile into the flute!

The Lessons in *Flute Time 2* start with a reminder about high D, which you met towards the end of *Flute Time 1*. High D is an excellent note to introduce you to the high register, so good luck—and take care!

DONE

Fingering diagram

Your teacher will explain this to you:

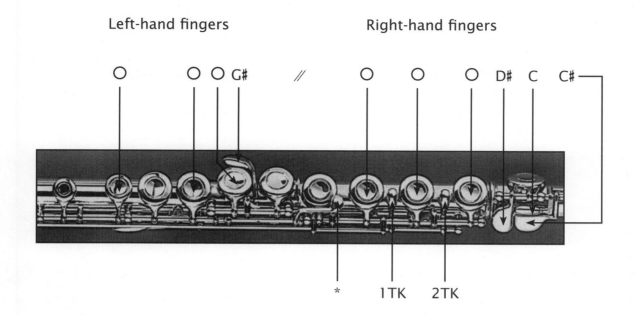

Left-hand fingers   Right-hand fingers

G#   //   D#   C   C#

*   1TK   2TK

Thumb keys

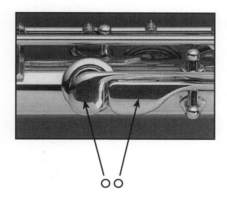

oo

●	press key down	○	leave key up
oo	Bb/B thumb keys	D#	press down D# key
G#	press down G# key	C#	press down low C# key
C	press down low C key	*	press down side Bb key
1TK	press down 1st trill key	2TK	press down 2nd trill key

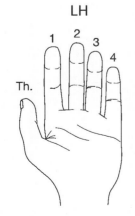

LH

1 2 3 4

Th.

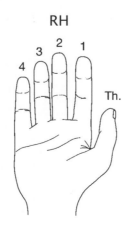

RH

4 3 2 1

Th.

This is how the fingers are described in the book—*not* the same as when playing the piano!

LESSON 1

High D: a reminder • ¢ time

GOAL

Remember that **high D** is really an altered low G. **Do not try to play it like low or middle D.**

Warm ups

• Practise both tongued and slurred.

La Donna è Mobile, from *Rigoletto*

Quick and bouncy ♩ = c.132–44

Giuseppe Verdi
(1813–1901)

Use thumb plate

Scales and arpeggios

Practise both tongued and slurred.

D major Scale (*across 2 octaves*); key signature F#, C#

D major Arpeggio (*across 2 octaves*)

D minor (**relative minor** of F major) Scale (*across 2 octaves*); key signature B♭

D minor Arpeggio (*across 2 octaves*)

8

* Reminder: Both your part and the accompaniment are given on track 2. Track 3 gives the accompaniment only. Please also see p. 5 of the Foreword.

If composers write 4 crotchets in a bar but want to suggest that the speed of the piece is very quick, they often write this time signature:

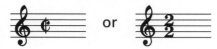

This time signature is known as **Alla Breve** time and means that you count 2 **minims** in a bar rather than 4 crotchets.

The Sheffield hornpipe

English trad.

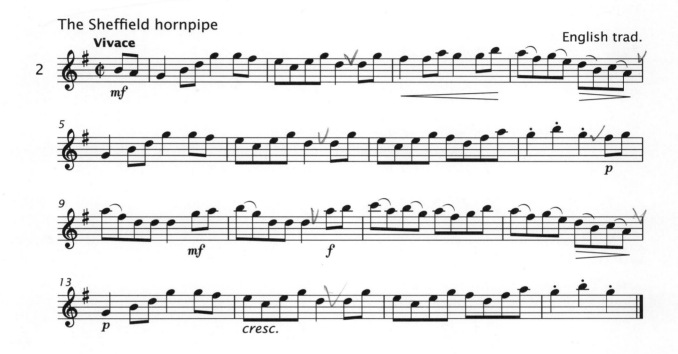

Shepherd's dance

Georg Philipp Telemann
(1681–1767)

DONE

For further practice of the points in this lesson, and all the lessons, see the suggestions in Appendix I, page 70.

The third fingering for B♭ •
The chromatic scale

GOAL

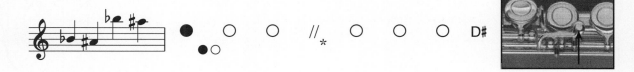

- This small key (arrowed) is a very useful key. It is played with the side of the RH 1st finger (against the top knuckle), not with the tip of the finger.

- When used with the fingering for B, it gives a low and middle B♭, useful in all sorts of situations, especially the chromatic scale. It is an alternative to the 'long' B♭ fingering you met in *Flute Time 1*.

- Obviously, this 'special' fingering cannot be used for B♭ when the notes either side of it use RH–1 normally (for example, F or E).

Teacher's note: To introduce this fingering, it's a useful idea to mark a + above every B♭ where you would like your pupil to use it (as shown below).

Warm up

- Play this several times until using the new B♭ key feels normal.
- Practise both tongued and slurred.

Falling down and climbing up the stairs

The Radetzky march

Johann Strauss I
(1804–49)

Here are two studies by Wilhelm Popp (1828–1903). Mark in the + for B♭/A♯ if you need to!

GOAL

The **chromatic scale** is a scale containing every semitone (a semitone is usually the smallest distance between two notes, for example, B♭ to B or F to F♯), rather like playing every note on a keyboard instrument, black and white. The word 'chromatic' comes from the Greek word 'khromatikos' meaning 'colourful'—the scale is certainly that!

In the chromatic scale, the important thing to remember is to use either the third fingering for B♭ or the 'long' fingering. Sliding the thumb between B and B♭ is lazy and does not make for good technique.

Here is the chromatic scale on G across 1 octave. You will normally see sharps going up and flats coming down:

The greasy pole

DONE

High E♭/D♯

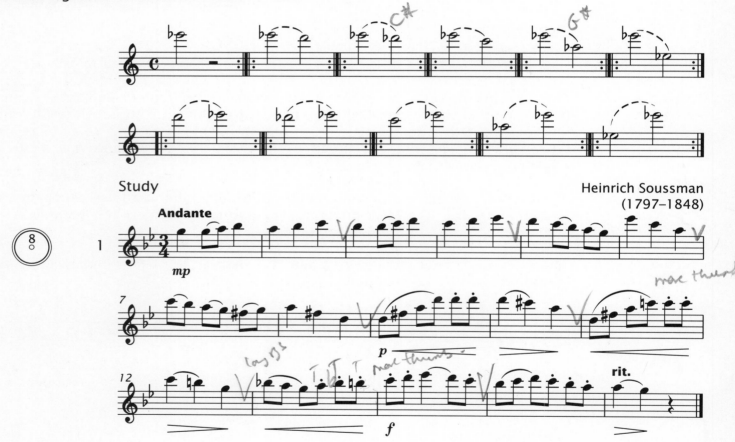

High E♭ (D♯) is such an easy note to remember—you put down every single finger, including both 4th fingers! **Don't play it like an overblown low E♭ (D♯)**—it's really an altered low G♯ (A♭).

Warm ups

- Practise each bar slowly, both tongued and slurred.
- Concentrate on smooth finger movement, taking special care to keep the fingers close to the keys as you leave high E♭.
- When you play up to the high E♭, aim for a well-channelled air-stream, especially when slurring, so that the higher note does not sound forced.

Study

Heinrich Soussman
(1797–1848)

Scale and arpeggio

In the E♭ major scale and arpeggio, make sure the LH–1 comes off for middle E♭ (indicated by an *). Notes within the brackets need carefully co-ordinated finger movement, especially in the RH. Practise slurred to test yourself!

E♭ major Scale (*across 2 octaves*); key signature B♭, E♭, A♭

Eb major Arpeggio (*across 2 octaves*)

London ladies, from *The Beggar's Opera*

John Gay
(1685–1732)

2

Cradle song

Johannes Brahms
(1833–97)

3

Ballade of the captives

4

DONE

High E

High E has a good, clear sound. **Don't finger it like low E**—it's really an altered low A. For high E, it's very important that the air-stream is angled correctly. If not, you will usually only get middle A, even with the correct fingering.

Warm ups

- Practise each bar slowly, both tongued and slurred.
- When moving up to high E, don't force the note: angle the air-stream carefully until the note emerges smoothly.
- Don't go on to the next bar until the previous one is really comfortable.

The Londonderry air
Andante ♩ = c.60–63
Irish trad.

1

p espress.

6

10

< mf

poco rall.

15

f

p

Dance steps
Not too fast

2

sempre f

5

14

A Yorkshire tango

Steady Tango Tempo ♩ = *c*.126–32

3

Little study, Op. 37, No. 2 (*adapted*)

Snatch a quick breath after every two bars;
let the dynamics rise and fall with the phrase.

Joachim Andersen
(1847–1909)

4

Scale and arpeggio

E minor (**relative minor** of G major) Scale (*across 2 octaves*); key signature F♯

E minor Arpeggio (*across 2 octaves*)

DONE

15

Low C and C#

Although some flutes have an extra key for low B, **low C** and **low C#** are the lowest notes on most instruments. They are played like low D plus one of the three keys for **RH–4**:

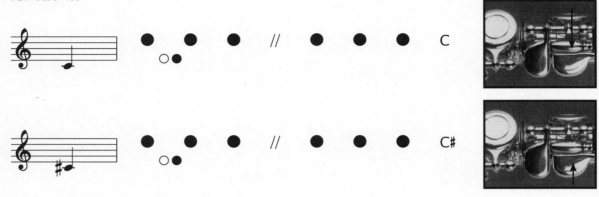

Occasionally you have to *slide* RH–4 from one little finger key to another, for example, when playing from C# and D#, from C to E, and so on. If you have very dry fingers, you can rub your RH 4th finger along the side of your nose (there is natural oil here) or put a spot of cork grease on the tip of RH–4—both methods make the sliding easier.

RH–4 should be *curved* when playing the D# and C# keys. Keep a straight little finger when playing the C key; it helps to keep only the tip of the finger on each of the three keys.

Warm ups

- Practise the fingering first, *especially the slides*; then play slurred and tongued.
- **NEVER leave RH–4 off the D# key for E and F**. Low D is the only note not requiring RH–4 to be down.
- Keep the lips relaxed and the air-stream moving forward; blow well into the flute.
- Don't leave any bar until it's absolutely correct in the fingers—be very strict with yourself!
- Try to keep your wrist still when moving from one RH–4 key to another.

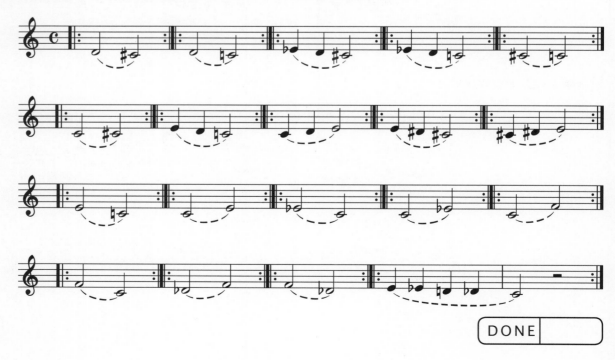

DONE

This exercise is based on one written by the famous French flute teacher, Marcel Moyse. The idea is that you descend slowly to low C, keeping a well-focused tone. The two places where you are likely to have to work hardest at this are when you land on low F and low D. Keep the embouchure relaxed.

Play fairly slowly, breathing where marked:

Warm up finger flourish

based on Jacques Offenbach
(1819–80)

The girl with the flaxen hair

Claude Debussy
(1862–1918)

Scale and arpeggio

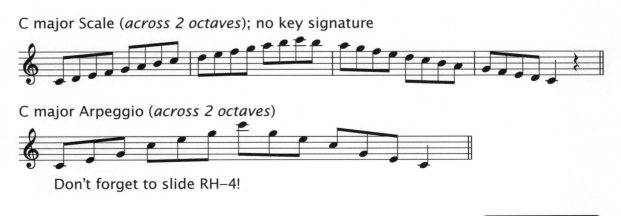

C major Scale (*across 2 octaves*); no key signature

C major Arpeggio (*across 2 octaves*)

Don't forget to slide RH–4!

DONE

9/8 and 12/8 time • 5, 7, and 8 time • Demisemiquavers

GOAL

In *Flute Time 1* you learned about 6/8—a **compound time** signature with two ♩. in each bar. 9/8 and 12/8 are also compound time signatures: 9/8 has three ♩. in each bar; 12/8 has four ♩. in each bar.

Duet: Pastoral scene

16

1 **Andante**

p

mp

f

poco rall.

p

Swap the parts around.

Cradle song, K350

Wolfgang Amadeus Mozart
(1756–91)

17 18

2 **Andante** ♩. = *c.*50

p

cresc.

p

p

p

rall.

p

The zither carol

Czech. folk tune

3 **Quick and bouncy**

p

f

p subito

DONE

Time signatures with **5**, **7**, or **8** as their top figure show bars with irregular beat groups.

5 time may be grouped:

7 time may be grouped:

Although **8 time** has exactly the same number of quavers as 4/4 (simple time), the notes are never grouped just in 2s or 4s. The most common grouping in 8 time is 3 + 3 + 2, giving a Caribbean flavour to the basic pulse:

Taking it easy

In the following tunes, a percussion instrument, such as a wood-block or drum, or even just a finger tapping the pulse, can be a big help.

Teacher's note: A slow-ish quaver beat is a good idea when pupils first tackle irregular metres. Then, as they become more confident, an increase in speed can be quite exciting!

Falling short!

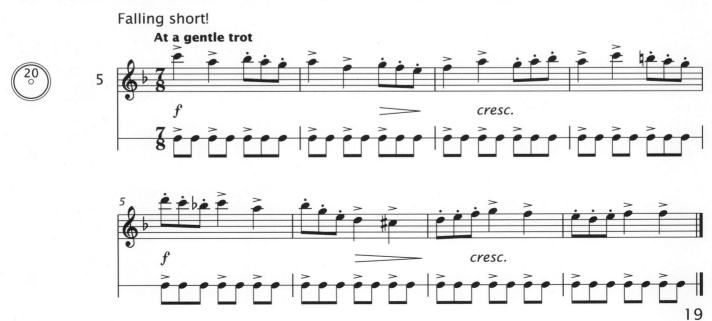

I feel giddy!

Caribbean steps

Five kicks

DONE

A **demisemiquaver** (or *thirty-second-note*) is worth an eighth of a crotchet. There are four to each quaver, two to each semiquaver.

On its own, it looks like this:

When grouped together in 2s or 4s, demisemiquavers look like this:

A demisemiquaver **rest** looks like this:

Composers tend to write demisemiquavers when they want the music to move quickly, though this depends on the speed of the basic pulse.

Warm up

• Clap then play, making sure that you fit notes exactly to the quaver pulse underneath!

Turkish march, from Sonata in A, K331

Wolfgang Amadeus Mozart
(1756–91)

Allegretto

LESSON 7

High F and F# • Syncopation

GOAL

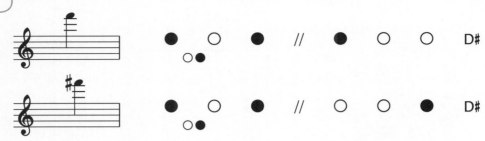

High F is really an altered low Bb. **High F#** is really an altered low B. As before, don't play them like overblown low register notes.

As high F# is really an altered low B, it can *never* be played with the Bb thumb on. It is a very good test of the embouchure and breath support—if you have any trouble, look again at The high register (on p. 6) and discuss with your teacher.

Warm ups

- Practise the fingers only to begin with.
- Practise both tongued and slurred. Slurring is a little trickier, therefore better for you!
- Wide ascending intervals will need extra care when raising and supporting the air-stream, especially going up to F#.
- Take special care co-ordinating the fingers when moving from high E to F and back. Keep fingers close to the keys.

Spring song, Op. 62, No. 6

Felix Mendelssohn
(1809–47)

Allegretto grazioso ♩ = c.126

22

South Cave market

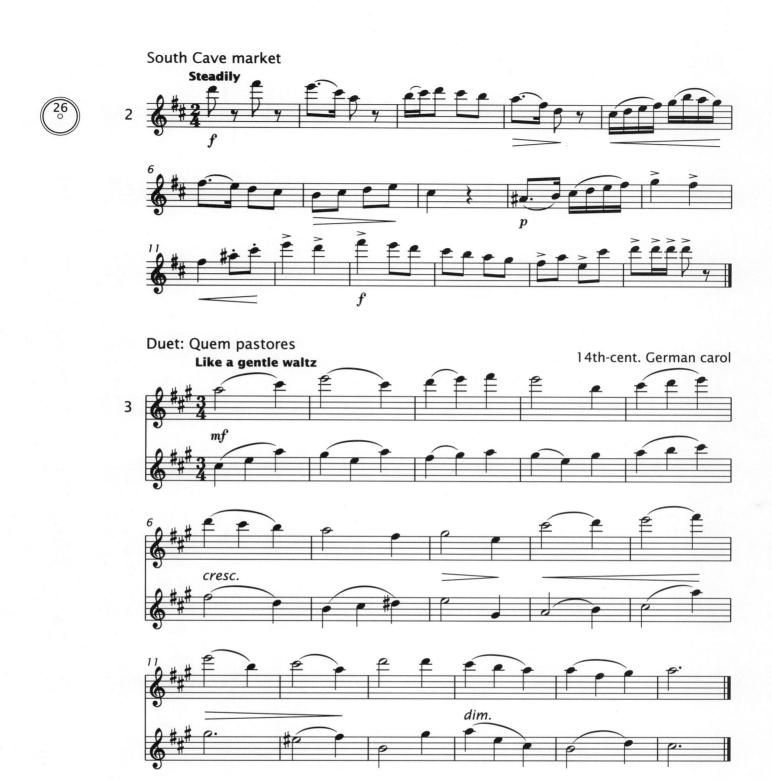

Duet: Quem pastores

14th-cent. German carol

Scale and arpeggio

F major Scale (*across 2 octaves*); key signature B♭

Practise high note fingerings first; try not to hesitate when you reach high C and D.

F major Arpeggio (*across 2 octaves*)

Study in F

Giuseppe Gariboldi
(1833–1905)

GOAL

Syncopation is a feature of rhythm where you play *off-the-beat*, that is, playing notes between strong beats. You've met this already in some of the tunes and exercises.

Here is a simple example; the second bar shows the placing of the syncopated notes in relation to the strong beats:

24

Syncopated rhythms can add a sense of urgency to a piece of music; they are also a strong feature of jazz styles.

Here is another example, showing how syncopated rhythms relate to strong beats:

Oxford rag

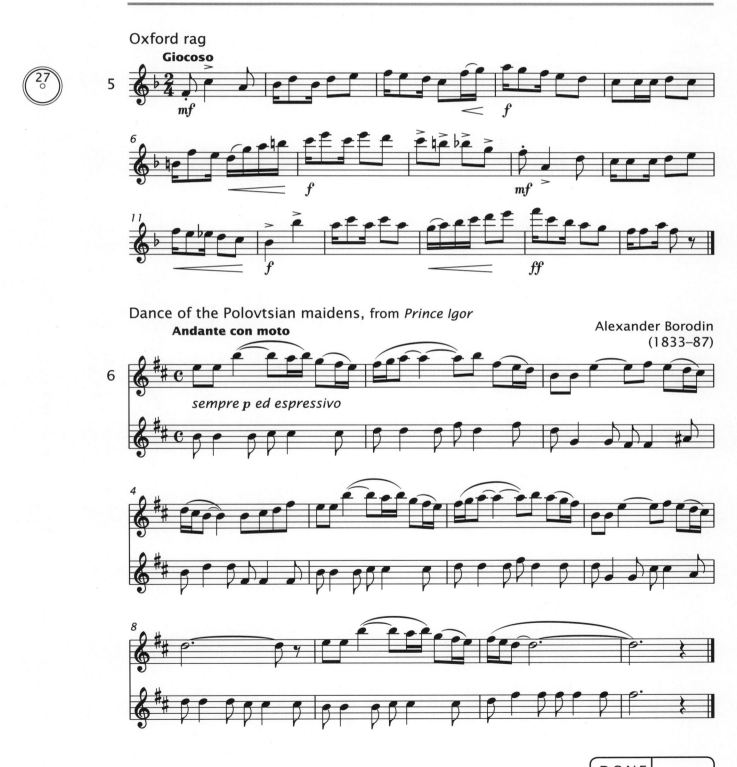

Dance of the Polovtsian maidens, from *Prince Igor*

Alexander Borodin
(1833–87)

DONE

25

High G

● ● ● // ○ ○ ○ D#
○○

High G is very similar in fingering to low G, but as it's really an altered middle C, the *thumb must be taken off*.

Warm ups

• Practise the fingers only to begin with. Co-ordinate them carefully, keeping them very close to the keys.
• Practise both tongued and slurred—the wider intervals will be most challenging!
• Don't force the sound—raise the air-stream gently!

All through the night

Andante con moto   Welsh air

Scales and arpeggios

G major Scale (*across 2 octaves*); key signature F#

G major Arpeggio (*across 2 octaves*)

G minor (**relative minor** of B♭ major) Scale (*across 2 octaves*); key signature B♭, E♭

If you normally use the B♭ thumb key, it must be off for all the notes within the bracket (high F♯ cannot be played with thumb B♭—see Lesson 7).

G minor Arpeggio (*across 2 octaves*)

Jamaica farewell

Caribbean trad.

Rhythmic ♩ = *c.*126

mf

mf cresc.

sf

Hava nagila

Hebrew trad.

Steady and deliberate

mp *cresc.* *f*

mp

p *cresc. poco a poco*

rall.

ff

DONE

QUIZ PAGES

All the answers are somewhere in the book. Try not to cheat by looking back!

1. Write in the note names:

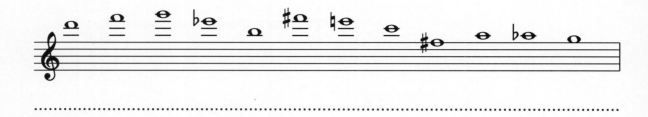

....

Write the same notes an octave lower:

2. How many s in the following: 𝅗𝅥. .... 𝅝 ....

♪. .... 𝅘𝅥 ....

3. Give the English for the following Italian terms:

Allegretto .... *ff* ....

Marcato .... **Molto vivace** ....

Con spirito .... *fp* ....

Grazioso .... *assai* ....

4. Is the $\frac{9}{8}$ time signature **SIMPLE** or **COMPOUND**? (Underline the correct answer.)

Write here two examples each of simple time and compound time:

Simple   **Compound**

28

5. Write in a time signature for this piece and fill in the missing barlines:

The key signature is B♭. Is the piece in **F major** or **D minor**? (Underline the correct answer.)

Why?...

6. Name these two scales:

....

....

7. Complete this exercise with your own rhythms in $\frac{5}{8}$ time, grouping the notes correctly:

8. What does ₵ mean? ....

What is the other way of writing it?

DONE

29

LESSON 9 — Phrasing • Articulation • Double-tonguing

GOAL

Phrasing

You will hear the word *phrasing* used a lot in music. It's a general term referring to what you do to a piece of music to make it really interesting and expressive.

Say a simple sentence like this in your ordinary voice: 'My name is . . . , I live in . . . , and I play the flute.'

Without having to try, your voice rises and falls naturally as you travel through the sentence. Now say it on a monotone, rather like a robot might—very boring and mechanical!

When you play, you colour the music using dynamics to achieve the same rise and fall, but you also have to decide where the musical sentences or *phrases* begin and end. This helps make sense of the music and also shows you where to place breaths, which for all wind players are the equivalent of punctuation marks (commas, full stops, etc.) in music.

Once you've decided on the phrases, you can add breath marks (usually shown by '), and think about shaping the melodic line with dynamics. All this helps make your playing interesting and holds the attention of an audience. With time and experience, choosing the right breathing places and shaping the phrases musically will become second-nature.

This well-known tune has ' marking breathing spaces and the ends of phrases, and dynamics to give the musical sentences expressive interest. Play it through, paying special attention to the breathing marks to get the feel of the phrase shapes and perhaps exaggerating the dynamics. Why do you think some ' are in brackets?

English country gardens

English morris dance tune

Here are two familiar tunes, but this time, *you* are the editor: you decide on, and mark in, phrase-lengths, slurs, dynamics, and speed. Make sure you can play all that you have written!

The trout

Franz Schubert
(1797–1828)

Toreador's song, from *Carmen*

Georges Bizet
(1838–75)

Both of these pieces have piano accompaniments, so don't forget to mark up the piano parts, too! Ask your teacher if you need some guidance.

DONE

Articulation

Throughout *Flute Time* you've been playing tunes and pieces with various patterns of tongues and slurs. The general term for this is *articulation*, which refers simply to how the music 'speaks'. This is just like ordinary speech, where, if you articulate clearly, it means your consonants are crisp and your vowels open.

You need to articulate clearly when playing the flute, and to do this the tongue has to be correctly positioned inside your mouth. Some players like the tongue to touch the gum just above the upper teeth; others like to bring it further forward to touch the teeth. Your teacher will guide you, but remember that to articulate with real clarity and speed you must have good, solid breath support.

Try not to let the tongue come between the lips; this is really a special effect to give a bell-like attack to slower notes and is no good for quick tonguing.

Here is the main theme from the overture *William Tell* by Rossini:

1. Play it through, not too quickly, tonguing every note. Is the sound a little tinny or brittle?

If so:

2. Play it again, but this time slowly, just *breathing*, *panting*, or *coughing* the notes using the support you would need for the word '*Hah*'—this is best for stirring your diaphragm into action!

If the notes are now reasonably firm in sound:

3. Play once more, again using the tongue, but making sure that every note has the same breath support.

Try not to disturb the embouchure when tonguing (especially quickly) and **never** let the sound of tongued notes, quick or slow, sound tinny or undernourished.

Important: some players try not to use the tongue at all when playing the flute and instead just use explosive little breaths, usually unsupported. Don't get into this habit! It's no use at all and prevents any sort of clarity, especially in quick music.

Mixed patterns of tongues and slurs
A key area to think about when combining tongues and slurs is *rhythm*.

When you tongue, the effect is to send the air along in a series of little movements. When you slur, the air comes out of you into the flute in an unbroken stream; the tongue is not there to act as a sort of 'braking' mechanism. Slurred rhythms may be uneven, especially if your fingers are not as controlled as they should be.

Take a simple group of notes and vary its tongues and slurs. Listen carefully to the slurred notes—are they all even? If you want to be certain, ask someone who understands to listen to your playing, or record yourself and listen back—you might get a shock!

Try these patterns:

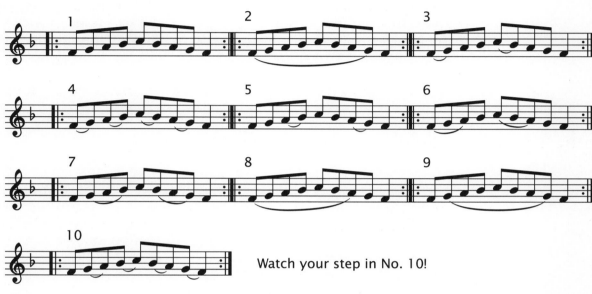

Watch your step in No. 10!

CHECKLIST

Don't leave each bar until you are happy with it.
• Are your tongues and slurs absolutely precise?
• Are you playing with even rhythm and all notes equally well-supported?

If not, **have another go**.

Now try these patterns an octave higher, but be careful not to disturb the embouchure.

F major was chosen because the fingers are fairly straightforward. Try the same patterns in other keys. Try to extend the range of notes to one or even two octaves.

'Pick and mix' features seven of the above patterns. Increase the speed when the articulation patterns are really exact.

Pick and mix

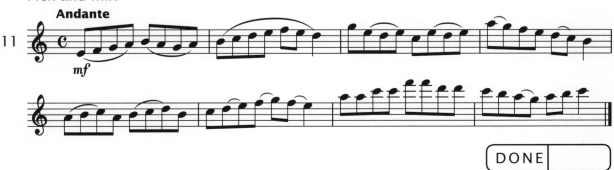

DONE

33

Double-tonguing

Up to now, you have been **single-tonguing**. This means using the tip of your tongue to articulate any notes which are not slurred.

However, when composers write music which is just too quick to be single-tongued, then we have to use **double-tonguing**. This means quickly taking the tongue forward and back so that you are using the syllables 'T–K' or 'D–G' instead of just 'T' or 'D'—this gives us a very rapid tonguing speed.

The embouchure must remain relaxed: double-tonguing can sound very tight and brittle otherwise, and you will find it difficult to keep your rhythm even. Taking the tip of the tongue a little further forward helps, if you don't do that already. Some players find 'D–G' less tight than 'T–K'.

The 'K' or 'G' stroke can be quite tight when you first start double-tonguing. One of my flute teachers recommended slow practice to help loosen up the 'K':

The object is to get the 'K' sounding just like a clean 'T'. You try.

As ever, it is firm breath support behind each stroke which helps to make this work. You don't need a flute to practise your double-tonguing: it can be done anywhere—on the bus or in the car!

Start with repeated notes at a fairly steady tempo. Increase the speed when you and your teacher are sure that the 'T' and 'K' both have a uniform strength and sound.

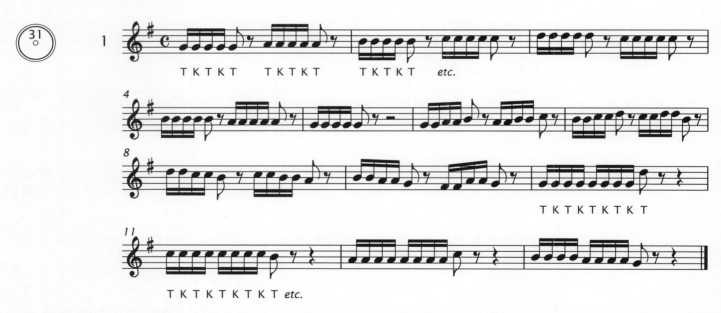

If you still have some difficulty, practise each note with 'K–K–K–K' (or 'G–G–G–G') to help reduce the resistance of this stroke, then with 'K–T–K–T'. Firm breath support really helps, but do have a break if your tongue gets tired—like the rest of you, its muscles need to be trained! Don't expect perfection immediately—it takes time.

Try the same exercise in different keys. Make sure that the tongue action does not disturb the embouchure, which must remain relaxed as you play higher. The 'Little study' by Andersen on p. 15 is good practice for this.

In the next exercises, take special care with the co-ordination between fingers and tongue. Keeping the fingers really close to the keys will help.

Vary the speed as you get more confident, and practise both *f* and *p*.

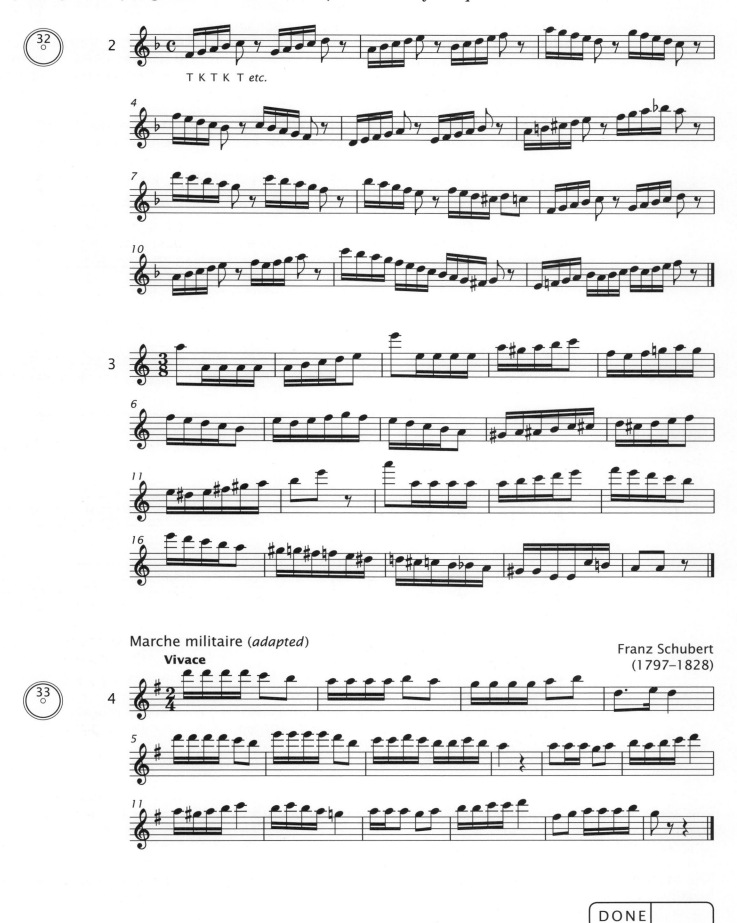

Marche militaire (*adapted*)

Franz Schubert
(1797–1828)

Vivace

DONE

Trills and other ornaments

Ornaments are shorthand signs that composers use when they want to decorate a melody. They're more common in the music of the Baroque and Classical periods (1650–1800), which was simpler in style than Romantic or Modern music (1800 to the present day).

The most common ornament is the **trill**. This tells you to play quickly from the note written to the note above and back for as long as the trill lasts.

The sign for a trill is *tr* written over the note, sometimes followed by a wavy line, which lasts as long as the trill:

Trills in the Baroque period (which includes composers like Bach, Handel, and Telemann) always start on the note *above* the one written:

* notice the extra C

Warm up

• Make sure that each trilled note has the full 2 beats.

When playing ornaments:
• Keep the fingers very relaxed and close to the keys. Any stiffness will slow you down, especially in the weaker fingers.
• Practise to strengthen the weaker fingers, but don't continue to practise if you feel any discomfort or pain in your fingers or hand. Little and often is the rule.

Some trills need special fingerings on the flute—see pp. 55–6.

The **acciaccatura** is a small note with a line through the stem and is crushed as quickly as possible against the note it decorates:

The **appoggiatura** is a small note which leans against the note it decorates. Its effect varies, but usually it halves the value of the main note:

This minuet by Mozart contains these three ornaments.

Minuet No. 1, from Sonata in C, K14

Tempo di Minuetto ♩ = c.120

Wolfgang Amadeus Mozart
(1756–91)

* These two appoggiaturas are played as ♩ ♩

Here are three other ornaments which you might meet, especially in Baroque music:

The **upper mordent**:

The **lower mordent**:

The **turn**. This can be played in three different ways:

It's your turn! Use the figures above as a guide.

DONE

37

High G# and A • Double sharps and flats

GOAL

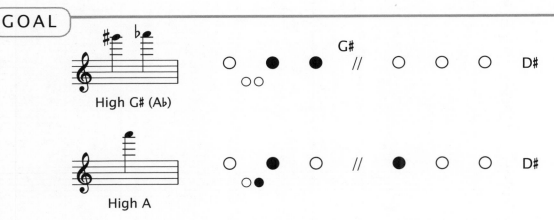

High G# (A♭)

High A

• **High G#** is really an altered open C#, so the LH thumb and 1st finger **must** be lifted.

• **High A** does not really resemble any other fingering, but the important thing to remember about it is that it is the last note in the 3rd octave which needs RH–4 on the D# key. Without this, it is hard to get and horribly sharp!

As these two notes respond very badly to incorrect fingering, it is **essential** to give them special care and attention.

Teacher's notes: High G# and middle D# are probably the two most vulnerable notes on the flute when it comes to leaving LH–1 down accidently. Because it's a difficult habit to break, you will need to be very vigilant, but the rewards are well worth it, especially when it comes to scales.

Warm ups

• Practise fingers only at first, then both tongued and slurred.
• It's very important that each bar is precise before you pass on to the next.
• Try not to force the sound to produce these notes—as before, keep the embouchure relaxed, raise the air-stream gently, and support each note firmly from the diaphragm.
• Keep fingers very close to the keys.

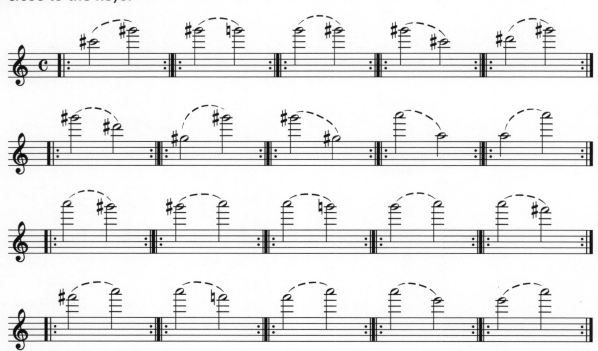

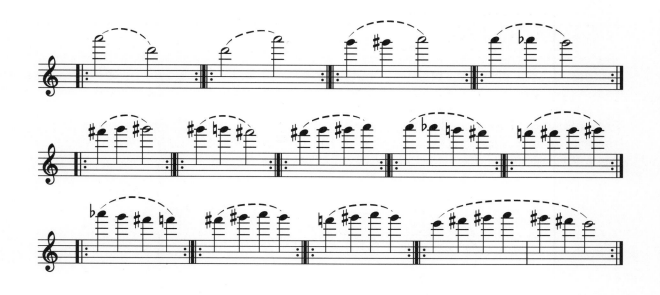

Go down, Moses

Andante

Spiritual

1

The Merry Widow waltz

Tempo di Valse ♩. = c.60

Franz Lehár
(1870–1948)

2

Scales and arpeggios

You may find the scales and arpeggios which start on G#/Ab and A a little tricky in the 3rd octave, compared with previous patterns, but if you have really got down to the exercises which begin this lesson and are comfortable with every one, there should not be a problem.

To begin with, focus your attention on the 3rd octave notes (starting on high D), just practising the fingers for now. Pay special attention to the fingering for top G#/Ab. When you come to blow, you will feel a lot happier if the fingers know what they are doing!!

A major Scale (*across 2 octaves*); key signature F#, C#, G#

Take special care moving up and down high E–F#–G#–A.

A major Arpeggio (*across 2 octaves*)

Slurring high E to A and back needs special care. Increase your air-speed as you ascend and vice versa.

A minor Scale (*across 2 octaves*); no key signature

Like A major scale, take special care moving up and down the top 4 notes.

A minor Arpeggio (*across 2 octaves*)

Slurring high E to A and back needs special care in this one, too!

Ab major Scale (*across 2 octaves*); key signature Bb, Eb, Ab, Db

Make sure that you lift LH–1 for both high Ab and middle Eb (marked with a *).

Ab major Arpeggio (*across 2 octaves*)

It will be very tempting to leave down LH–1 for the notes marked * in the arpeggio— take care! Also, make sure that you do not leave down the G# key for more notes than necessary!

A **double sharp** (✗) next to a note does just that—it **sharpens** the note twice. A **double flat** (♭♭) **flattens** it twice.

Look at this piano keyboard. You will see that if you sharpen the note **F** twice, it becomes **G**. If you flatten the note **B** twice, it becomes **A**.

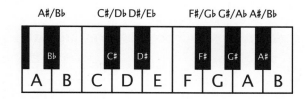

As an example, look at the scale of G♯ minor (**relative minor** of B major):

You will notice that each F has a ✗ next to it. Why not just write G? The main reason is that a normal major or minor scale (known as a 'diatonic' scale) cannot have the same letter of the alphabet twice, so the G has to be renamed **F✗** as we already have **G♯**.

To restore a double sharp or flat note to an ordinary sharp or flat, write:

or sometimes:

To restore either of them to a natural note, write:

or sometimes:

Seeing double

DONE

High B♭ and B

GOAL

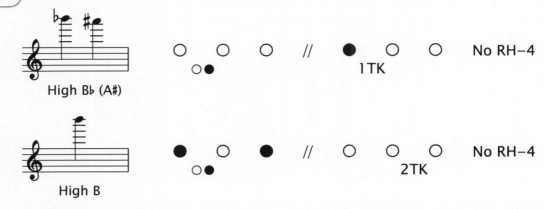

- **High B♭ and B** are the only notes on the flute to use the **trill keys** as part of their normal fingering. You should take RH–4 **off** for both notes—they can be a little difficult to get if you leave it down (especially B).

- **High B♭** uses the **1st trill key** (**1TK**), played with **RH–2**.
  LH–1 is normally **off** for this note, as, with middle D♯, there may be an undertone if it is left down.

- **High B** uses the **2nd trill key** (**2TK**). This is normally played with **RH–3** (the finger you use for F♯), but in some places (B major and minor arpeggios especially) you need to play it with **RH–2**. High B can *never* be played with the B♭ thumb key on.

When you see **high B♭** or **B** coming up, get into the habit of positioning RH–2 or RH–3 over the 1st or 2nd trill keys as soon as you can—don't be taken by surprise! This is best done when you are practising the fingers alone.

HINT

Practising these finger positions in front of a mirror really helps.

Warm ups

- As usual, practise fingers first, then play tongued and slurred.
- To avoid playing sharp, don't tense the lips—keep the embouchure relaxed and raise the air-stream only slightly.
- Never turn the flute in to help get the highest notes! It causes weak tone and serious intonation problems.

For high B♭

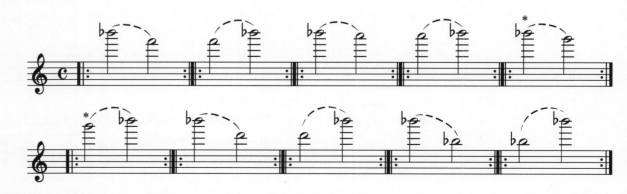

* Playing from high B♭ to G and back needs care—the balance between hands feels unsteady at first.

For **high B**

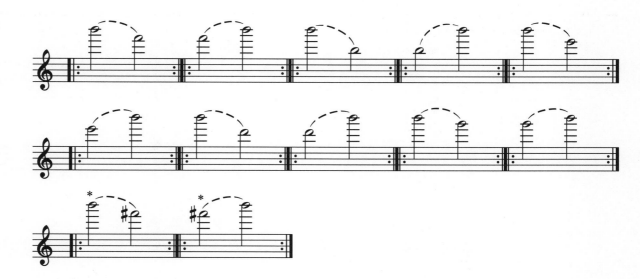

* For these last two bars, use **RH–2** on 2TK for the high B and **RH–3** for the high F♯.

Playing from high B♭ to high A♭ and back needs particular care with both finger co-ordination and the balance between the LH and the RH:

• Make sure that RH–4 is **off** for **high B♭**, but **on** for **high A♭**.
• Make sure that LH–1 stays **off** for both notes.

In the following three exercises, you have to slide the trill key finger to and from its adjacent key. It's rather a clumsy thing to have to do, but there's no way round it, so try to make it as neat as possible:

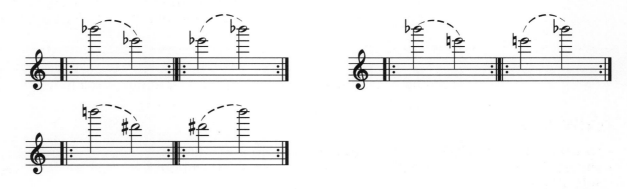

There's a lot to think about when playing from **high B** to **high A** and back:

• Make sure that RH–4 is **off** for **high B**, but **on** for **high A**.
• There is considerable finger movement involved here, so co-ordinate fingers carefully, keeping them as close as possible to the keys.

DONE

The butterfly

1

Study

Giuseppe Gariboldi
(1833–1905)

2

Scales and arpeggios

Bb major Scale (*across 2 octaves*); key signature Bb, Eb

Bb major Arpeggio (*across 2 octaves*)

B major Scale (*across 2 octaves*); key signature F#, C#, G#, D#, A#

B major Arpeggio (*across 2 octaves*)

Light Cavalry overture

The high Bs in bars 22 and 30 will need to be played with RH–2:
take care with the stretch back to A.

Franz von Suppé
(1819–95)

DONE

Top C • 8ᵛᵃ indications

GOAL

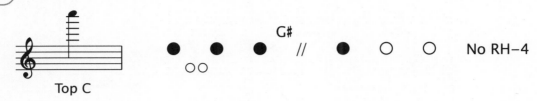

Top C

Although it's possible to play a few more notes above it (see Fingerings: Trills and extra-high notes on p. 55–7), **top C**, a very exciting note, is normally regarded as the highest one on the flute. Well done—that's all 37 of the flute's notes covered!

You can see that top C has rather an unusual fingering: it feels a little like an F and a high G♯ combined, but there are two important things to remember about it: RH–4 is **off** (the note can be very difficult to produce if you leave RH–4 down on the D♯ key) and the LH thumb is also **off**.

Warm ups

• Along with all the highest notes, it's very important not to turn the flute in to help get top C! As usual, keep the air-stream raised and support firmly from the diaphragm.
• Don't leave any bars until you and your teacher are satisfied with the quality of the top Cs.

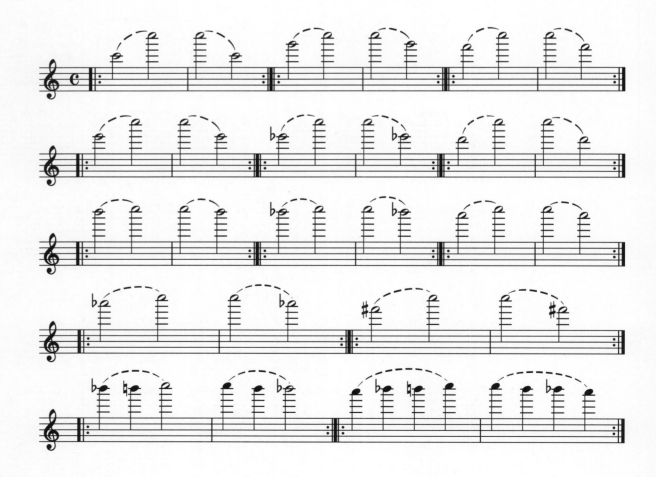

An **8ᵛᵃ indication** is a shorthand sign that composers use to show that the notes must be played an octave higher than written:

is played as:

8ᵛᵃ indications are not so popular with flute players because we get so good at reading notes on the ledger lines! And besides, as the high notes are fingered so differently from the low ones, we prefer to see them written in their proper place.

Some composers write the word *loco* (an Italian word meaning 'back in place') when they want to cancel an 8ᵛᵃ indication.

High jump

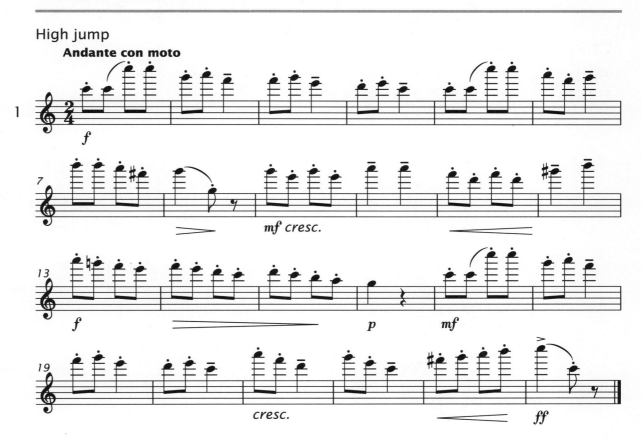

A little study

Concentrate on really close, even fingers; don't force the sound.

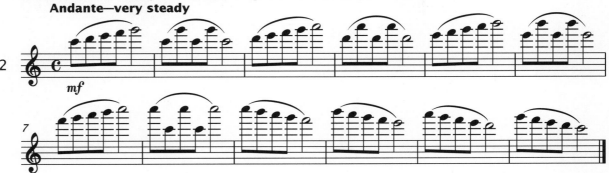

47

Maple leaf rag

Scott Joplin
(1868–1917)

Tempo di Marcia ♩ = *c*.66

Rhythm workout • Composing with modes

GOAL

Throughout *Flute Time 1* and *2* you've met and used various rhythmic patterns. This lesson draws some of these patterns together and gives you the chance to show that you can keep them going against a steady pulse—essential when playing with others.

To get the best from the workouts, you need to play alongside at least one other person, preferably a lot more than one! There are three workouts, in simple, compound, and irregular time.

Practise the individual rhythms at home; then, in the lesson with your teacher or fellow pupil tapping the pulse, select a line and try to keep the rhythm going against the steady pulse. If there is more than one of you, you could play different notes in each line to make up chords. You could also practise the rhythms at home against a metronome.

If you can, listen to a recording of *Clapping Music* by Steve Reich; I guarantee you'll be very impressed!

1. Simple time

2. Compound time

3. Irregular time

DONE

GOAL

In *Flute Time 1* you composed some tunes in major and minor keys; here now is a chance to compose using **modes**. Modes are very beautiful forms of the scale, with the semitones in different places. They were in use for many hundreds of years and became popular again in the 20th century.

The scale you know as the major scale is also the 1st mode, known as the **Ionian** mode, with the semitones between the 3rd and 4th, and the 7th and 8th degrees. This table shows all the modes and where the semitones are:

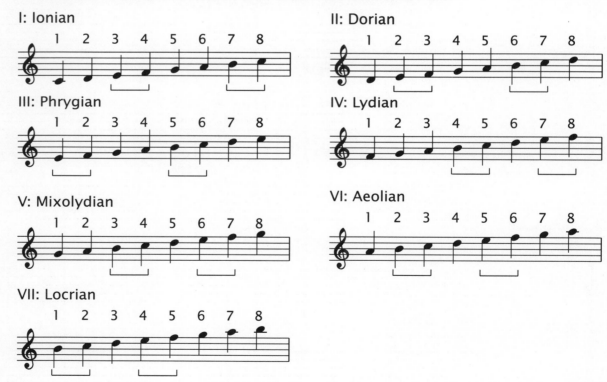

If you want to write, for example, in the **Lydian** mode starting on F without key signature, you would have to finish on the note F to establish this mode. It might seem odd to finish on the note F when there have been no B flats in the piece, but this is what makes modes so interesting!

1. Play this short piece in the **Phrygian** mode:

Title: . . . .

You'll notice that it sounds rather like a sad folksong. Can you think of a title for it?

2. Play through the modes to get a feel for their character and colour. You can vary the mood of your pieces a lot depending on which mode you use. The **Locrian** mode is very much the odd one out because the distance from its 1st degree to its 5th is not like any other. Ending a melody in the Locrian mode will always sound unfinished!

3. Here now are some blank staves for you to try composing with modes. Choose the mode you like best, pick a time signature, and away you go!

DONE

WARM UPS AND HARMONICS

Warm ups

Building up stamina is very important when learning a wind instrument, where the hands, and also the facial and abdominal muscles, are all used.

The key to success is **regular practice**; you'll find a regular daily session is much more use to you than practising only two or three times a week (or less!). Regular practice gives you time to absorb each new piece of information and develop the stamina and confidence to put it across convincingly.

Here are some tips:

1. Practise at the same time each day. Try getting up extra-early to practise before going to school!
2. Practise willingly and in a good mood. If you're feeling grumpy, begin with a piece or short exercise you really like, and go from there. You'll almost always find you can then practise a lot more cheerfully.
3. Warm up first and, once you're into your practice, don't waste time playing what you can play already. Focus on what is tricky for you and work through that. It's best to start with long notes, then scales and arpeggios.

So, play this to put a smile on your face:

And away we go.

Warm-up jingle 1: No problems

Warm-up jingle 2: Take care!

In the next one: 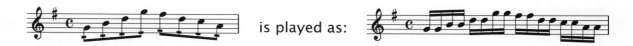 is played as:

This is good practice for double-tonguing.

Warm-up jingle 3: Loosen your tongue!

Listen to the quality and uniformity of your tone in these warm ups:

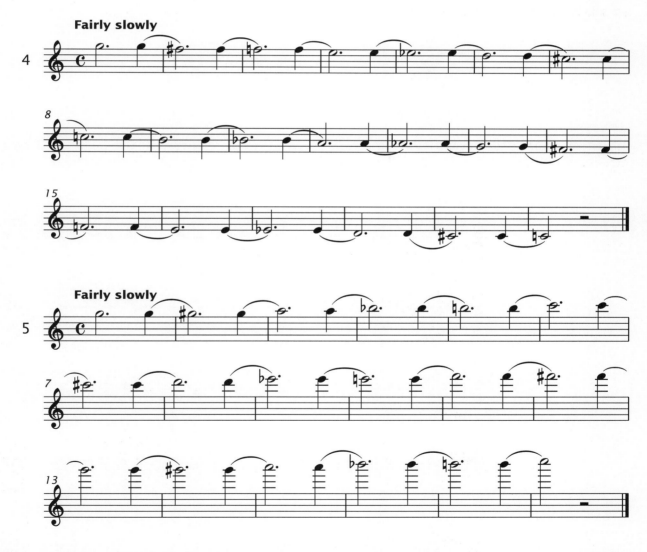

These five warm ups make part of a very good warm-up routine. Make up your own warm-up routine, perhaps writing some warm ups of your own.

DONE

Harmonics

Harmonics are all the notes you can produce from low note fingerings just by raising the air-stream. They are used only rarely by composers as a special effect, but are very good for other reasons, warming up especially, and helping to train your embouchure to produce a firm air-stream. And as they are naturally a little out-of-tune, they help to develop your musical ear also.

From low C, it's possible to produce all these notes:

Try to produce these notes yourself and see how far you can get. High B♭ and top C are usually a bit reluctant!

The large low C is known as the **fundamental**, the small notes as the **harmonics** or **upper partials**. The 2nd harmonic provides most of the middle register. The 3rd harmonic is the most used as a special effect; the 4th occasionally.

Composers show harmonics either by small diamond-shaped notes above the fundamental, or by a small circle over the note, when you have to decide what the fundamental is:

Try these exercises. Keep playing the fundamental notes, easing out the harmonics by raising the air-stream. NB: 'Long' B♭ will not work as a harmonic in No. 5—use the B♭ thumb key instead.

54

DONE

Trills and extra-high notes

Low and middle register

Trilling to a semitone or tone above the written note uses standard fingerings most of the time. Two trills are not possible: Low C–D♭ and Low C#–D#. Trills which need special fingerings are given here.

Trill the key(s) arrowed.

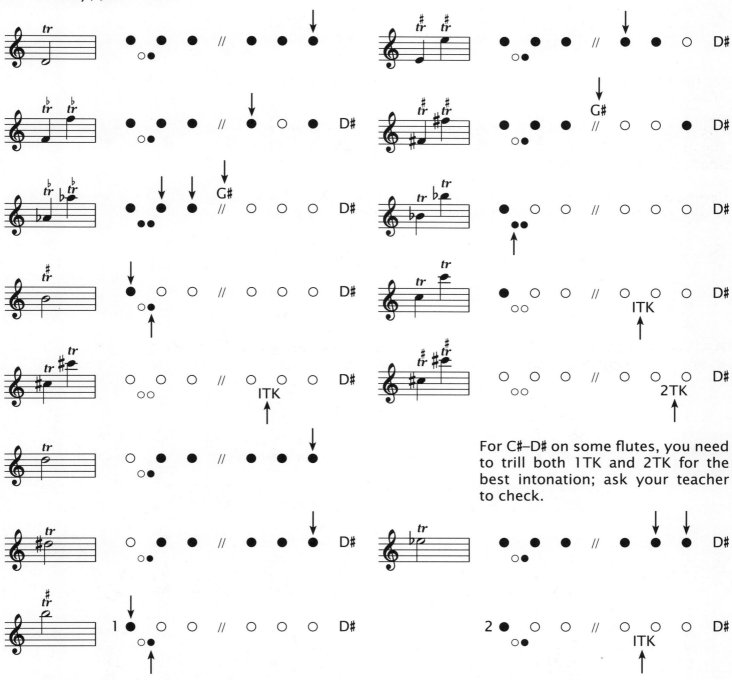

For C#–D# on some flutes, you need to trill both 1TK and 2TK for the best intonation; ask your teacher to check.

The high register

The trill fingerings are all irregular and there is often more than one choice. Some of the highest may not work, depending on the response of the flute.

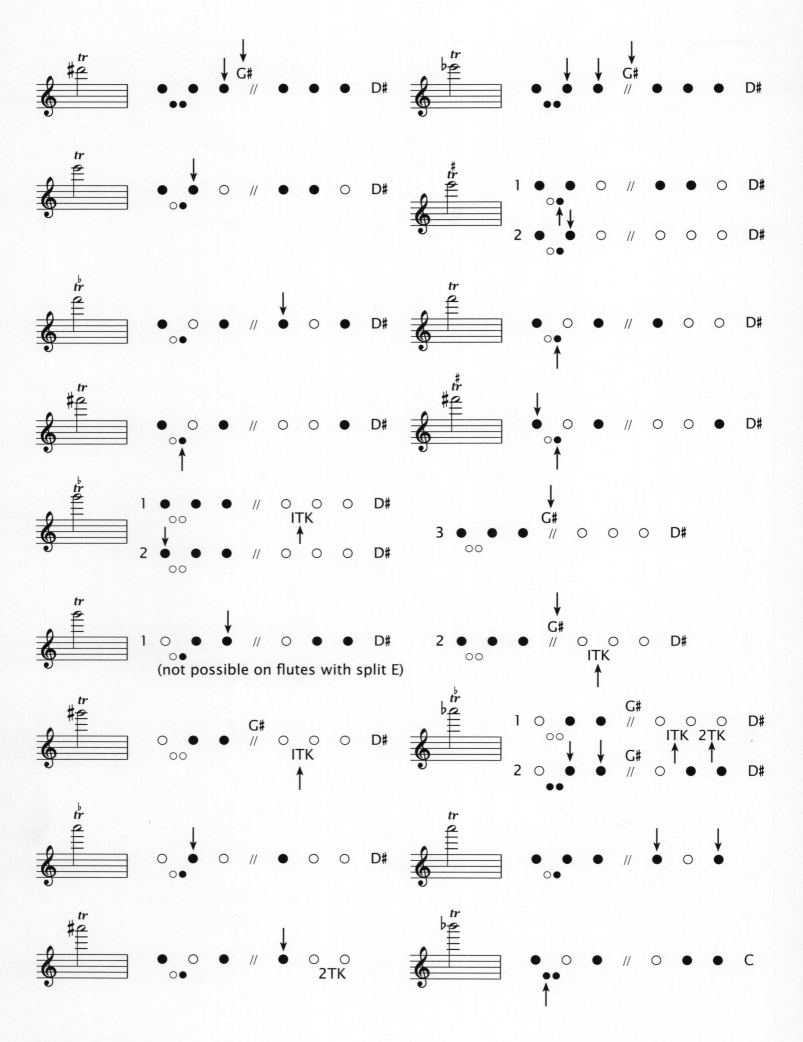

56

Extra-high notes

With improvements to instruments over the last 150 years, the range of the flute has extended above the C, although the notes above top D are used only rarely. Try them by all means, but don't spoil your embouchure!

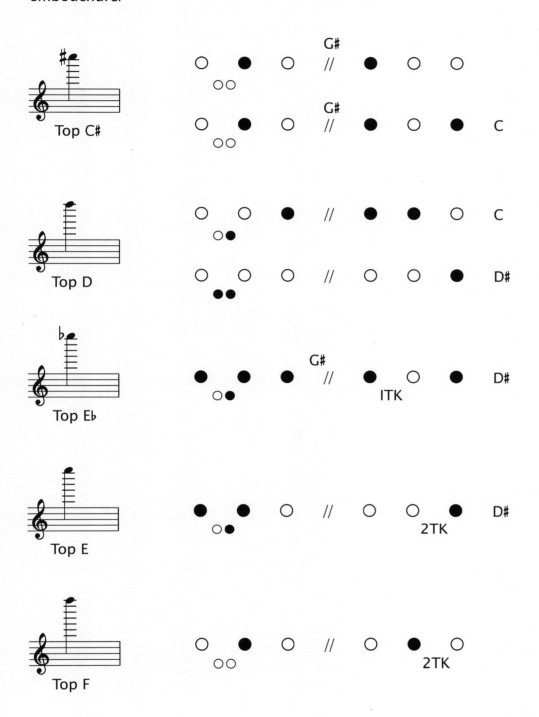

MELODIC MINOR SCALES

Along with a good sense of rhythm and a well-focused tone, the ability to play all your scales and arpeggios well is a vital part of being a musician. They really are the building blocks of all you play, and if you know them well all your other activities on the flute—pieces, studies, sight-reading, composition, improvisation—are always much easier and more rewarding.

So far, the minor scales you've played have been **harmonic** minor scales, which have the same notes ascending and descending. The **melodic** minor scale is a little different. When you *ascend*, the 6th note is a semitone higher than the 6th note of the harmonic minor scale:

D harmonic minor (*across 1 octave*)

D melodic minor (*across 1 octave*)

The melodic minor scale changes on the way down to the notes of its **relative major** (you'll remember that each major and minor key are related). The relative major of D minor is F major, so D melodic minor *descending* looks like this:

Here is the complete D melodic minor scale across 2 octaves:

Play these melodic minor scales on A, E, and G. The * show the differences from the harmonic minor scale. Can you work out by ear the melodic minor on F?

A melodic minor (*across 2 octaves*)

E melodic minor (*across 2 octaves*)

G melodic minor (*across 2 octaves*)

DONE

58

CHECKLIST

How are you doing?

Place a tick in the box if you have covered all the following points well. Make sure that your teacher ticks the other box if he or she agrees. If there is still an area which needs working on, go back over it following these and your teacher's suggestions.

	Pupil	Teacher
You now know the 37 notes of the flute's standard range. Do you feel equally comfortable producing all of them? Be honest, especially about the very high notes. *Revise exercises recommended by your teacher from each lesson.*	☐	☐
Are you fingering all notes correctly, especially middle D♯ and the top five? *Revise exercises recommended by your teacher from the necessary lessons.*	☐	☐
Is your tonguing really clear and do you cope well with different articulation patterns? *Check your breathing, and practise scales and arpeggios with different articulations.*	☐	☐
Is your tongue/finger co-ordination really safe? *Practise selected exercises, scales, and arpeggios, keeping fingers very close to the keys.*	☐	☐
Are you able to play rhythmically, holding a steady beat in all time signatures? *Revise exercises selected for you by your teacher, preferably with a metronome. Revise the Rhythm workouts in Lesson 14.*	☐	☐
Do you think hard about *phrasing*, that is, the way you colour and shape your playing? *Revise Lesson 9. Try to give your musical imagination more freedom.*	☐	☐
Can you hear well-phrased playing from other people? *Listen to as many performances as you can, both recorded and live.*	☐	☐
Is your intonation really improving? *Ask your teacher's opinion! Listen especially carefully to the pitch when you vary the dynamics and be aware of the tricky notes on the flute: middle C♯, high E, high F♯, high G♯, high B, and top C—all usually a little sharp; the lowest notes, middle E♭, and high B♭—usually a little flat.*	☐	☐
Are you breathing deeply using the entire capacity of your lungs? *Revise breathing technique with your teacher.*	☐	☐
Are your compositions developing imaginatively? Can you play them? *Try to give them a sense of structure but don't be afraid to be adventurous!*	☐	☐
How are your scales and arpeggios? Do you understand how scales and modes are built? *Revise the necessary pages.*	☐	☐
Have you planned a routine of warming-up and practising? *Talk this over with your teacher. Aim for daily practice.*	☐	☐

DONE ☐

CONCERT PIECES AND STUDIES

Here is a very fine movement from a sonata by Telemann. The upper line is known as the *urtext*, the original that Telemann wrote. The lower line is a *realization*, that is, an example of how you might perform it bearing in mind the Baroque style.

Sonata in F major, 1st movement, TWV41: F2

Georg Philipp Telemann
(1681–1767)

Here are a few suggestions for slurs and dynamics in this siciliana by Bach. Add some of your own, trying to keep them consistent.

Use 'long' B♭ in this short study and take special care where you place the slurs.

This study, taken from Drouet's *Méthode* of 1827, is in one of the most beautiful keys for the flute. Place breaths carefully and aim for the best range of expression you can manage without disturbing the intonation.

Study in C# minor

Louis Drouet
(1792–1873)

Symphony No. 5, Minuet and Trio
MINUET

Spanish dance, Op. 12, No. 4

Moritz Moskowski
(1854–1925)

fiero = proudly

D.C. al Fine

Short study No. 2

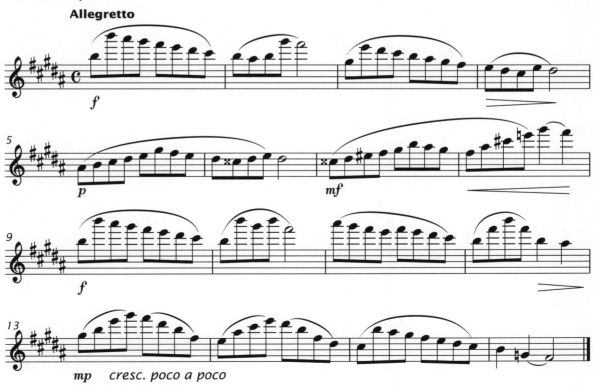

FREQUENTLY ASKED QUESTIONS

Q **I find some of the high notes very difficult to produce. What can I do about this?**

A: First, ask your teacher to check that your flute has not sprung a leak underneath one of the pads. This happens sometimes on instruments which have adjusting screws and will need sorting out by your teacher or a competent repairer—don't try to do it yourself!

Secondly, don't forget that the high register notes need *easing* out: your lower jaw has to move slightly forward so that you produce a faster, raised air-stream. Don't think about 'blowing harder'—that's fatal. Make sure that you are providing plenty of breath support, keep the lips relaxed, and don't take the note up until it's ready to move naturally and freely. And of course, *do use the correct fingerings*!

Finally, you will find high notes difficult if *you* are out of condition, that is, if you practise only rarely. You must build up stamina to play the flute well, and if you miss a day or two (or, in the holidays, a week or two!), much of the good work you have done is wasted and you have to build up your stamina all over again. A regular dose of long notes—low, middle, and high—is usually the best remedy, but you must be patient.

Q **I find it difficult to play in time and keep up with others. How can I improve this?**

A: Go back over the simpler exercises, paying special attention to the pulse and how the rhythms fit against it. Playing to a metronome is a good idea, as the pulse is provided for you (if you don't have one yet, ask your teacher's advice about which to buy). And of course, play with other people as often as you can.

Q **I find scales and arpeggios difficult to learn. Is there an easy way?**

A: First, don't leave scales and arpeggios to a hasty last-minute scramble before an exam—this is not treating them with respect! Practice sessions should be organized so that scales and arpeggios (whether you have an exam or not) come second after some long notes or warming-up exercises; you will then find that pieces can be learned so much more quickly.

Here are some tips for practising a tricky scale—let's take B major as an example:
- Practise fingers silently first.
- Look at all the places which are likely to be a challenge. In B major, the top two notes involve the *trill keys*; the scale also has high F♯ and G♯ which need special care; make sure that the balance between hands feels comfortable between high G♯ and A♯; use the 'long' or 'special' fingering for middle A♯—no B♭ thumb in this one! Slurring from middle G♯ and A♯ needs care; and of course, lift LH-1 for middle D♯!
- Play the scale slowly in minims. If you go wrong, stop at that point and immediately put it right—fingering first, then try the few notes either side of the problem area; don't waste time by going back to the beginning of the scale. Make sure that you are raising the air-stream carefully from middle E onwards.

Q **I have got into a few bad fingering habits. What should I do?**

A: Throughout *Flute Time 1* and *2* there are exercises designed to help prevent this—you must have shot through them too fast! With your teacher, select the exercises to revise and eradicate any problems.

Q **I get out-of-breath very quickly in some music. How can I hold notes for longer?**

A: First, check that the opening between your lips is not too large and that your lower lip is well forward. Oddly enough, some people have difficulty with this because they forget to take in enough breath to begin with. Always prepare to play with a slow, leisurely breath where possible and never breathe at the last moment, if it can be avoided.

Remember that the combination of a well-formed embouchure and good, solid breath support do nearly all the hard work for us.

Q **How can I improve my tonguing speed?**

A: This is not just about the speed of the tongue, but its position in your mouth, whether or not you are giving it firm support from the breath helping to propel it forward, and keeping the embouchure relaxed.

Like any other aspect of flute-playing, tonguing needs to be practised for itself. Single notes, scales, and arpeggios are ideal for this as you should not have to spend too much time worrying about the printed page, leaving you free to experiment with differing patterns of tongues and slurs (see Lesson 9). You can't really improve your speed if you only practise tonguing as you meet it in your pieces.

It's important not to turn to double-tonguing until you and your teacher are happy with the quality of your single-tonguing.

Q **I would like to produce a more beautiful tone. What's the best way?**

A: Good breathing is responsible for nearly all we do on the flute, and that includes making a fine sound. Always check your breathing first and your fingering second if there are any problems.

Another reason why you might not be getting the sort of sound you want is that you may have outgrown your instrument. Beginner flutes are usually made of silver-plated nickel and some people believe that this may limit the possibilities of tone and response as your playing becomes more advanced. Headjoint design is also an important factor to consider.

Flutes made of solid silver (and other precious metals) and wood cost a lot of money, so a good compromise solution is to buy a handmade solid silver headjoint to fit the flute you have been playing on (assuming it to be in good tuning and mechanical order). This will certainly increase your potential, but don't forget that it is *you* that makes the good tone—that splendid silver headjoint only helps!

There are many specialist shops where you can spend hours trying out hundreds of headjoints. These places are only too happy for you to do this and if you choose one of their headjoints, they will fit it for you for free. As ever, your teacher's advice is all-important.

The other option is to buy a good, second-hand professional flute—there are lots of these about, too, but buying one without advice can be dangerous, especially as they might not come with any warranty. Again, ask your teacher to help.

Q **My ambition is to be a professional flute-player. What do you advise?**

A: It's very important to be realistic about this. The professional music world is very competitive: obtaining, for example, Grade 8 with Distinction, although a high standard, does not mean that you are to be the next James Galway or William Bennett. The standard of students entering music college has risen enormously over the last 30 years.

First, compare your current playing standard with those of players of the same age. You can do this by attending one of the many holiday courses for flute-players which take place throughout the country, mostly in the summer. These courses feature public master-classes and individual tuition with eminent teachers. Consider joining the British Flute Society for all the latest news in the flute world (www.bfs.org.uk); its journal *Pan* lists all courses worldwide.

If you want a more detailed, frank opinion of your chances, ask for a consultation lesson with a flute professor at one of the music colleges you are thinking of applying to. He or she will be very experienced at assessing potential and will let you know exactly how you stand. Your current teacher will be able to access details of colleges and their professors.

Additional recommended studies

This appendix lists useful additional material which can supplement the pieces and exercises given in *Flute Time 2*. Details of publishers etc. are given at the foot of p. 71.

Lesson 1

Ben-Tovim: *The Young Orchestral Flautist*
Book 1: Nos. 1, 11, 17; Book 2: Nos. 11, 14, 29, 35
Bullard: *50 for Flute*
Book 1: Nos. 16, 17, 19, 23
Moyse: *24 Small Melodious Studies*
No. 3 (theme and 2 variations)
Stokes: *Easy Jazz Singles*
Nos. 8, 9, 17
Vester: *125 Easy Classical Studies for Flute*
Nos. 36, 43, 66
Vester: *100 Classical Studies for Flute*
Nos. 6, 7, 15, 19

Lesson 2

Ben-Tovim: *The Young Orchestral Flautist*
Book 2: Nos. 16, 27, 36
Bullard: *50 for Flute*
Book 1: No. 22
Stokes: *Easy Jazz Singles*
Nos. 24, 25
Vester: *125 Easy Classical Studies for Flute*
Nos. 68, 77, 78

Lesson 3

Ben-Tovim: *The Young Orchestral Flautist*
Book 2: Nos. 25, 39, 40
Bullard: *50 for Flute*
Book 1: Nos. 21, 26
Vester: *125 Easy Classical Studies for Flute*
No. 59
Vester: *100 Classical Studies for Flute*
No. 9

Lesson 4

Ben-Tovim: *The Young Orchestral Flautist*
Book 2: Nos. 1, 2, 12, 20, 21, 22
Bullard: *50 for Flute*
Book 1: No. 30
Hunt: *63 Easy Melodic Studies for Flute*
Nos. 22, 23, 24
Vester: *125 Easy Classical Studies for Flute*
Nos. 25, 38, 44, 48
Vester: *100 Classical Studies for Flute*
Nos. 14, 22

Lesson 5

Wye: *Practice Books 1 & 2*
Book 1: Exercises on pp. 7–9 involving low C and C#;
Book 2: Exercises on p. 6

Lesson 6

Ben-Tovim: *The Young Orchestral Flautist*
Book 2: No. 38; Book 3: No. 3
Bullard: *50 for Flute*
Book 1: Nos. 15, 25
Harris & Adams: *76 Graded Studies for Flute*
Book 1: Nos. 32, 44
Stokes: *Easy Jazz Singles*
Nos. 19, 21

Lesson 7

Ben-Tovim: *The Young Orchestral Flautist*
Book 1: No. 12; Book 2: Nos. 9, 44A, 45, 48;
Book 3: Nos. 5, 14, 21, 28, 33, 43
Bullard: *50 for Flute*
Book 1: No. 28
Hunt: *63 Easy Melodic Studies for Flute*
Nos. 27, 28, 29, 52
Lyons: *Progressive Flute Studies*
Nos. 11, 16
Moyse: *25 Etudes Mélodiques*
Nos. 1, 2
Vester: *125 Easy Classical Studies for Flute*
Nos. 15, 49, 51, 56, 83, 117

Lesson 8

Ben-Tovim: *The Young Orchestral Flautist*
Book 1: No. 14; Book 2: Nos. 23, 30, 44B, 50;
Book 3: Nos. 6, 16, 34, 38, 41, 46
Bullard: *50 for Flute*
Book 1: No. 29
Harris & Adams: *76 Graded Studies for Flute*
Book 1: No. 38
Hunt: *63 Easy Melodic Studies for Flute*
No. 47
Lyons: *Progressive Flute Studies*
No. 22
Stokes: *Easy Jazz Singles*
No. 33
Vester: *125 Easy Classical Studies for Flute*
Nos. 26, 57

Lesson 9

Ben-Tovim: *The Young Orchestral Flautist*
  Book 2: Nos. 4, 49; Book 3: No. 17, 30, 33, 35
Bullard: *50 for Flute*
  Book 1: No. 20
Hunt: *63 Easy Melodic Studies for Flute*
  No. 24
Hunt: *45 Progressive Melodic Studies for Flute*
  Nos. 35, 36, 37
Moyse: *24 Small Melodious Studies*
  Nos. 1, 2, 6, 7 (theme only)
Platonov: *30 Studies for Flute*
  No. 3
Vester: *125 Easy Classical Studies for Flute*
  Nos. 31, 58, 59, 60, 108, 125
Wye: *Practice Book 3*
  Exercises on pp. 10–24 inc.

Lesson 10

Ben-Tovim: *The Young Orchestral Flautist*
  Book 2: Nos. 15, 31, 41; Book 3: No. 1, 7, 12, 13, 22
Hunt: *63 Easy Melodic Studies for Flute*
  Nos. 35, 36, 37, 38, 39
Vester: *125 Easy Classical Studies for Flute*
  Nos. 52, 53, 54, 55

Lesson 11

Ben-Tovim: *The Young Orchestral Flautist*
  Book 3: Nos. 8, 9, 18, 20
Bullard: *50 for Flute*
  Book 2: Nos. 32, 35
Harris & Adams: *76 Graded Studies for Flute*
  Book 1: Nos. 40, 43, 46
Hunt: *45 Progressive Melodic Studies for Flute*
  Nos. 10, 21
Platonov: *30 Studies for Flute*
  Nos. 2, 6, 11
Wye: *Practice Book 1*
  Exercises on pp. 18–21, going no higher than A

Lesson 12

Ben-Tovim: *The Young Orchestral Flautist*
  Book 3: No. 42
Bullard: *50 for Flute*
  Book 2: Nos. 37, 39
Hunt: *63 Easy Melodic Studies for Flute*
  Nos. 56, 57, 58, 59, 60, 61
Platonov: *30 Studies for Flute*
  Nos. 8, 15
Wye: *Practice Book 1*
  Exercises on pp. 18–21 not covered in Lesson 11

Publishers

Atarah Ben-Tovim, ed.: *The Young Orchestral Flautist*
  Book 1 (Pan Educational Music PEM 110)
  Book 2 (Pan Educational Music PEM 111)
  Book 3 (Pan Educational Music PEM 112)

Alan Bullard: *50 for Flute*
  Book 1 (Associated Board 2495)
  Book 2 (Associated Board 2496)

Paul Harris and Sally Adams, ed.: *76 Graded Studies for Flute,* Book 1 (Faber)

Simon Hunt, ed.: *63 Easy Melodic Studies for Flute* (Pan Educational Music PEM 34)
Simon Hunt, ed.: *45 Progressive Melodic Studies for Flute* (Pan Educational Music PEM 33)

Graham Lyons: *Progressive Flute Studies* (Hunt Edition 27)

Marcel Moyse: *24 Small Melodious Studies* (Leduc)
Marcel Moyse: *25 Etudes Mélodiques* (Leduc)

N. Platonov: *30 Studies for Flute* (Anglo-Soviet/Boosey & Hawkes)

Russell Stokes: *Easy Jazz Singles* (Hunt Edition 36)

Frans Vester, ed.: *125 Easy Classical Studies for Flute* (Universal 16042)
Frans Vester, ed.: *100 Classical Studies for Flute* (Universal 12992)

Trevor Wye: *Practice Books 1–3* (Novello)
  Book 1: Tone
  Book 2: Technique
  Book 3: Articulation

APPENDIX II

Enharmonics

C = B# = D♭♭	E♭ = D# = F♭♭	F# = G♭ = E✗	A = G✗ = B♭♭
C# = D♭ = B✗	E = F♭ = D✗	G = F✗ = A♭♭	B♭ = A# = C♭♭
D = C✗ = E♭♭	F = E# = G♭♭	G# = A♭	B = C♭ = A✗

Italian words

This is a fuller working list of Italian words than you met in *Flute Time 1*. It is by no means exhaustive and you will come across many more terms (including some French and German ones), especially when you study theory.

f (*forte*) loudly ** *ff* (*fortissimo*) very loudly ** *mf* (*mezzo forte*) moderately loudly

p (*piano*) quietly ** *pp* (*pianissimo*) very quietly ** *mp* (*mezzo piano*) moderately quietly

crescendo/cresc. (or ◁) getting louder ** *fp* (*fortepiano*) loudly, then immediately quietly

diminuendo/dim. (or ▷) getting quieter ** *sf* (*sforzando*) strongly accented (forced)

\> accent the note (similar to *sf*)

accelerando (accel.)	getting faster
Adagio	very slowly
agitato	with agitation, excitedly
alla marcia	in the style of a march
allargando	broadening the pace
Allegretto	not quite as fast as **Allegro**
Allegro	quickly
Andante	at a walking pace
Andantino	slightly faster than **Andante**
animando/animato	becoming more animated
appassionato	passionately
assai	much or very much (e.g. **Allegro assai**)
A tempo	back up to speed
attacca	straight on, without pausing
calando	decreasing in both speed and volume (dying away)
cantabile	in a singing style
con brio	brilliantly
con forza	with force
con fuoco	with fire
con moto	with motion/movement
con spirito	with spirit
deciso	decisively, resolutely
decrescendo/decresc.	getting quieter (same as *diminuendo*)
delicato	delicately
dolce	sweetly
dolente/doloroso	sadly
D.C. (Da Capo) al Fine	repeat from the beginning to the word **Fine** (the end)
D.S. (Dal Segno)	repeat from the sign 𝄋
espressivo	expressively
giocoso	joyfully
giusto	exact (e.g. **A tempo giusto**— return to exact tempo)
Grave	slowly and solemnly
grazioso	gracefully
Largamente	broadly
Larghetto	slightly faster than **Largo**
Largo	broadly (dignified)
legato	smoothly
leggiero	lightly
Lento	slowly
L'istesso tempo	stay at the same speed
Maestoso	majestically
marcato	stressed sharply
marziale	in a military manner, martial
misterioso	mysteriously
moderato	moderately (usually added to other words, e.g. **Allegro moderato**— moderately quickly)

morendo	dying away
ossia	alternatively (indicates an alternative version of a passage of music)
perdendosi	dying away
pesante	heavily
(a) piacere	freely, as the performer pleases
Prestissimo	extremely fast
Presto	very quickly
quasi	almost, as if
ritardando/ rallentando (rit./rall.)	slowing down
risoluto	resolutely
ritenuto	held back
ritmico	rhythmically
rubato	freely ('robbed', where time is taken from one value and given to another)
scherzando	playfully
semplice	simply
sempre	always
senza	without
smorzando	dying away
sostenuto	sustained (often implying a slowing of the tempo)
staccato	short, detached (shown by a ♪)
stringendo (string.)	pressing on, becoming faster
subito	suddenly
Tempo primo	return to the original tempo
tenuto (ten.)	held (a stress on a note, often shown by a ♩)
tranquillo	calmly
troppo	too (as in **Allegro ma non troppo**— lively, but not too much)
tutta forza	as strongly as possible
vigoroso	vigorously
Vivace	lively
Vivo	in a lively manner

qualifiers

meno	less
molto	a lot
più	more
poco	a little

(these words are usually added to other words, e.g. **molto rall.**— slow down a lot)

72